About the Author

Samual Karlin is a disabled veteran of the U.S. Coast Guard turned poet by very fortunate circumstances that took cathartic writing and made it into something beautiful. He lives with his fiancée and their dog Ozzie. Samual is a first-time author hoping for a grand future in the realm of poetry and fiction. He works in the information technology field at the college he attended for some time and which helped hone rampant thoughts into poetry.

Thinking of You

Samual Karlin

Thinking of You

Vanguard Press

VANGUARD PAPERBACK

© Copyright 2023
Samual Karlin

The right of Samual Karlin to be identified as author of
this work has been asserted by him in accordance with the
Copyright, Designs and Patents Act 1988.

All Rights Reserved

No reproduction, copy or transmission of this publication
may be made without written permission.
No paragraph of this publication may be reproduced,
copied or transmitted save with the written permission of the
publisher, or in accordance with the provisions
of the Copyright Act 1956 (as amended).

Any person who commits any unauthorised act in relation to
this publication may be liable to criminal
prosecution and civil claims for damages.

A CIP catalogue record for this title is
available from the British Library.

ISBN 978 1 83794 080 6

*Vanguard Press is an imprint of
Pegasus Elliot Mackenzie Publishers Ltd.*
www.pegasuspublishers.com

First Published in 2023

**Vanguard Press
Sheraton House Castle Park
Cambridge England**

Printed & Bound in Great Britain

To Kasey, without whom I wouldn't have had the muse or the confidence to put this together. You are my forever, always. They told me to choose happiness, so I chose you.

04/30/2022

Looking into your eyes
is like seeing the earth alive
awakened by a sunrise.

Gratuity

I wish I knew how you did this;
made me love doing something I thought I hated.
Maybe that just makes you good at your job,
what do I know?
You gave me means to create something,
what did you ask for in return?

Prayer

I don't know what comes next.
But when I find out I'll let you know
if I can

if I can

if I could, I wouldn't have been so selfish

I don't know what comes next
but I've done the best I can
the best that I could.

I know it was flawed all the while
quite flawed
broken and bent
but isn't that just the human condition?
No, not the way I did it.
So fundamentally wrong,
even you of love and forgiveness should scorn me,
in a way I hope you do.

You should
you should
maybe you already did.

And that is what led me here.
Flawed from the onset
serving this specific purpose
no, I'll buy that. How much do you want for it?
My life?

Sold.

I'm Overthinking!

And the thing is
I know exactly what I'm doing
what I did
what I did
what I'm doing.

And for no reason,
real or imaginary,
should I be analyzing
and thinking
contemplating
tearing apart word for word
every little interaction.

And for no reason
should I not be
ecstatic
for the
ecstasy
you generate.

Yet here I sit,
in my little skull-encased hell
holding my tongue,
scrutinizing the words
yet to leave my lips.

You're Wrong

I know what you're thinking,
that somehow,
this hiccup,
brief conundrum
is dire and death-dealing.

I know what you're thinking,
and you're wrong.
I see it in your eyes.
I can feel it.
You're disappointed,
and wrong.

Please, I know what you're thinking.
But can I just say…?
You are enough;
you are enough
for me.

Porsche 911

Into knots
I have tied myself,
the anxious ball of gray matter
has grasped the wheel...
leaving me in this
sweltering uncontrollable state.

3.8 seconds is all it took
for me to go from nothing
to a word I won't say.

I never got to tell you
how I truly feel
but I think you figured it out.
You're smart.

You knew how to get
exactly what you wanted from me.
All that was left in the air
was how, when and would I.
And I did.

Here I am spiraling

down a corridor
I know all too well.
Spiraling towards a feeling
I just want reciprocated by someone
just once.

I thought briefly
that maybe you might
and all would be well.
But that is just
part of the problem isn't it.
You let me inside and I plotted a future.

3.8 seconds is all it took
for me to go from nothing
to a word I won't say.

Some part of me wishes
I had let it slip.
Maybe this would be
different.

Maybe I wouldn't be trapped
in my head
had I been forthcoming
with my feelings.
Maybe none of this is even real.
Perhaps
just maybe,

I misread the whole situation
and in actuality
and in reality
I am just thinking
over thinking
over thinking
over thinking
which is really the trap
that I set for my own foot.

3.8 seconds is all it took
for me to go from nothing
to a word I don't want to say.

None of This is Real

none of this is real
none of this is real
none of this is real
none of this is real!

I have to bellow
against the voice
in my head
that demands dissonance.

I have to bellow
against the voice
in my head
that tells me
you're playing games.

So easily I could
let slip
my grip
and float in
agony
alongside the current.

So easily I could
let slip
my grip
and succumb to
the anarchy
my brain cell houses.

'None of this is real'
I whisper to nothing
and no one
but myself.

But what if it is?
and once again,
I have ruined something
before it could walk
on its own.

But I bellow anyway,
to no one
and nothing
and for no one
but myself.

None of this is real,
please believe me.
I'm terrified though,
but never have I felt
more alive.

So I distance myself;
I pull back
and play my own game
all the while
swearing,
praying,
up and down that you wouldn't.

None of this is real.

Pieces

I saw my whole life reflecting
in the screen of an iPhone
so against the wall
I shattered it
And now I'm lying on the floor in pieces.

Patterns

You see them in nature
so why not me?

I thought this one would be different
that somehow, I would succeed
where I had fallen
every time before.

Send me a sign.
Send me down a line,
I'm calling from the bottom
but you don't hear me.
Just meet
me in the middle,
I am a refugee.

But I fall back
into my same pattern
evidenced by this pen
and the ink it spills.

There was a time
when I shut off
everything
and let the lizard brain drive.
I sometimes wish
that was my reality
instead I am
a bleeding heart,
and I want to be yours.

But I fall back
into my same pattern
evidenced by this pen
and the ink it's spilling.

And I wonder,
will you come for me?
And break this spell
all while casting your own.

Just Another Love Poem

I told myself to never write one.
That putting this kind
of energy into the universe
was like asking to have you
ripped away.

But I feel compelled,
like you're behind me
controlling my fingers
in this moment.

You could tear me to pieces;
skin and bone,
and I would be grateful
just to be in your
presence.

Having you as my
own is more opulent
than ever I dreamed
possible.

And no, this isn't
a confession
of a feeling I'm
not ready to announce.
But I hope
you'll change that.
I want to
say it more than
I want to breathe.

Because I see a good thing
here.
I hope you do too.

If Life is a House

then I am just a guest living in the room
poised high above the garage
and no one else is near.

If life is a house
then who chose these decorations
clinging to every inch…
nothing is clear here.

Is it broken and divided?
Sturdy and tall?
Duplex or single family?
You don't want my answer.

If life is a house
then I am just a guest living in the room
wandering from vacancy to vacancy
playing not a key part at all,
a supporting character in my own story.

If life is a house
I would share it with you, I think,
there's another room down the hallway.

I would put you there if I could,
will you give me the chance?

Is it broken and divided?
Sturdy and tall?
Duplex or single family?
I might change my answer.

If life is a house
will you help me decorate?
Change the lens
and maybe the paint
but definitely the pillows.

If life is a house
it feels less empty now
you're barely moved in though,
will you stay a while?

If life is a house
if life is a house
if life is a house
you make it a home.

I Am Not a Perfect Lover

I get attached too easily
and have to hold back my tongue
from saying things that
I know I feel
but can never tell if you feel the same.

I am not a perfect lover,
I let my mind get the best of me
taking over and making
me think I have nothing
to love in the first place.

Wait.
That might be too strong a word
but there is something
in the back of my mind
that says that maybe,
just maybe,
it is the appropriate word
and I have been going about this all wrong.

I am not a perfect lover,
your eyes make me anxious

because I get lost in them
and you won't draw me a map
any time I get the gumption
to steal a glance
only to find that you're
already matching me.

I am not a perfect lover
I'm overthinking the simplest
word choice
with that one thing
that I need
to say.

Just three little words,
do you dare me to say them?
We both know that I want to,
but are they what you want to hear?

I Like the Way You Look (At Me)

'I like you,'
you said.
It hung in the air
enthralling my feeble mind
and now all I can think
about is you.

There's a song that goes
something like
the way you look tonight
but I think it could be improved.
I would say it's not about how you look tonight
I would say it's about how you look at me.
I would say it's the way your eyes soften
when you look at me.
When you look at me,
when you look at me I get dizzy.

'I like you,'
you said.
It hung in the air
enthralling my feeble mind
and now all I can think

about is you.

'You're trouble,'
I say,
your glistening gems for eyes
like pills in the right light
offering intoxication
on a level I can't really even
fathom.

'I want you,'
you said
and it sent shivers down my spine
because I thought I would die alone
and maybe I will die alone
but not tonight.
Tonight,
'I love you,' you said.

Fallen

I still fall for you
like suns do for skies.

And I'm scared
that you'll lose faith.

But I've fallen,
I don't ever want to get up.

Except into your arms,
for there is where I feel the most myself.

I still fall for you,
I didn't know I could go this far.

But here I am,
falling for you with every new glance.

I know,
I wear my heart on my sleeve.

But I put it there,
so you could find it.

I Think I Found My Place

and that is in your arms.

I once
only expected to die alone.

But here you are,
changing my mind
making it yours
and yours alone.

A degenerate
that you plucked up
and made your own
so effortlessly.

I am yours
I am yours
I am yours and never
will I be shared.

05/13/2022

I don't know
how else to put this.
But I know you're worried
and I want to ease that.
Tell me the secret,
share with me the spell,
I want to cast that from
your mind.

There's so much I want,
but nothing more
than to make you happy.

Your worries are mine,
and my shoulders can bear
the weight.
Just share them with me
and together,
we'll conquer the world.

Tell Me Why Everything I Write is About You?

What will it steal from me this time?
There's just no fucking hope in sight.
I'll make it through the night
But not my heart, not my heart,
And I knew from the get-go
That I feel too much, I over love.

But this time is different.
I'll die up on that hill.
Don't tell me
you don't feel it too.

This time is different.
You're my only drug,
my only vice,
my only type.
I've fallen for you
and it feels right
it feels right
it feels right.

They say unicorns don't exist,
but then how do they explain you?
I burn for you
I burn for you
I burn for you
and no one else.

Three Little Words

I am not a perfect lover,
sometimes I have too many drinks
and I worry too often.

'But I love you,' you said.
I had been wanting
to tell you
to tell you
to tell you,
and you beat me to it.

I am not a perfect lover,
sometimes I overthink what I say,
and I'm self-conscious.

'But, I love you,' you said.
And all of that went away.
The world lifted
and I saw a light
I didn't know existed.
I am not a perfect lover,
sometimes I get too emotional,
and feel immature.

'But, I love you,' you said.
and all of that went away.
And now all I can think
about is you.

I love you too.

You

I remind myself of you, in daylight, when
I miss you and cannot reach across the bed

for the comforting filling and refilling
of your chest. What a scintillating aspect
to my life you have presented. You lay there
looking as beautiful as the moment

I saw you. The moment that I fell in love
with you. The moment that I knew
forever my life would be changed
entirely, for only the better. You
are the missing piece that had evaded
and left me emptied. But now

with you I am whole. And one day, maybe,
hopefully, you'll say those two little words.

A Shovel

come here.
let me help you
bury our pasts.
and let them
fertilize our future,
together.

Today

I found purpose
in the folds of your smile
and the ever sparkle
in your eyes when
they fall upon me.
I am just watching you breathe,
learning that happiness
could be so filling.
Just a daily dose of my appreciation
for your existence.

Constructs

Let's push on
I won't take it slow.
They say,
we're moving too fast,
I said,
when you know you know.

This little thing
on all their wrists
tells them I'm out of control
but what does it know?

Just a construct,
a man-made idea
that I can't believe in
now that I have you.

I knew the moment
I laid eyes on
the folds of your smile
that I would have
a question to ask you.

So let's push on
love, I don't want to
take it slow.
Because now I know.

Disability

They all call me broken,
disabled,
in pieces
shattered
from the hand life
dealt for me.

But they all forget
I have you
and thus
I am more whole
than ever I have been.

06/20/2022

Our future is so very bright,
I wake up to
its blinding light
with a smile
upon every morning,
rolling to see your soft breaths
fill my life.

Broken

I am not broken like you
and you are not broken like me.

And yet our shared past
makes our future as clear
in my mind as the sky
after a storm.

I am not broken like you
and you are not broken like me.

Broken
Broken
Broken
but together, whole.
Our pieces together fit
like lost and battered
jigsaw pieces.
Together, whole.

I'm Ready

I've made up
my mind this evening.

It feels like a lifetime ago,
that I would've taken the last
drink to solidify my mind.

But now I know all
that poison does
is kill something inside
that I'm too fearful
to confront.

I've made up
my mind this evening.
All without the
liquid confidence
I used to think I needed.
But the strength to go
without,
you've granted me
graciously.

Stigma

I saw the look in your eyes when I told you.
I still see it. It's burned into my memory bin.
It haunts me like a ghost without the 'boo!'

I saw the look in your eyes when the medicine kicked in, boo.
I still see it. The reflection of disapproval towards this mannequin.
You should have just given me the shoe.

I saw the look in your eyes when it halted us two.
I still see it. Makes me feel worth less than tin.
Maybe I should just have blamed the brew.

I saw the look in your eyes, my head went askew.
I still see it. Never will it make me anything but chagrin.
Felt like you had run me through.

I saw the look in your eyes, not quite what you wanted to ensue.
I still see it. It feels more like I should've had some gin.
Makes me think my body has plotted a coup.

I saw the look in your eyes when I couldn't live up to the
    sneak-preview.
I still see it. I don't know what to do about this evil within.
Shit, I just wish I had turned blue.
But oh no, instead here's to solidarity, just me without you.

Galaxies

I never really liked brown eyes.
And I imagine some say
yours are simply that.
But they don't see
the galaxies hiding in yours
that I know are there.
I never really liked brown eyes
until yours fell upon me.

The Ravens Who Watch the Dawn by the Stones

Huginn and Muninn
the eyes of the god
watch the suns and stars arise
in your eyes
as the dawn welcomes
the new day.

Huginn and Muninn
the wisdom of the All-Seer
watch the suns and stars set
in your eyes
upon our problems
as each close and
lay the slate clean.

Inquiries

I have a question to ask.
It's a simple binary.
Yes or no.
But I'll admit,
I prefer an affirmative.

We used to shoot the shit,
and talk about this very moment.
You told me how you'd answer,
so why am I shaking
in trepidation
like I'm shitting razor blades?

I feel like I know your response,
I really do,
and it excites me.
My shaking turning from
terror to towering
excitement
for what comes next.

Stay

You are the only hope for me,
am I the only hope for you too?
So stay with me
and don't take
that hope away.

I go to pick up the phone
every day.
I miss you all the time,
because you are the only
hope for me.

And I pray that
you aren't just
passing through.

You're Going to Push Me Away

aren't you?
Am I no different
from the rest?
You get in these moods
where you don't want me around
and then
you ask me to move in,
and I can't help but wonder
how that will work.
I am beyond excited
to take this step with you,
but I can't help but wonder
am I no different from the rest
and you're going to push me away
like them?

I Can't Keep Losing You

It's all in my head.
Every night I lose you.
In my nightmares,
you're the one walking away.
I can't keep losing you
and I don't know how
to get over this anxiety.
Unlike suns do for skies,
don't fall away.
I hear your voice
when I sleep at night,
and more times than not
it lies to me
and says I'm not good enough.
But I want to be.

Soulmates

I know we said
we don't believe in them.
But I think I would
always find you
if nowhere else,
then in my dreams.

Flailing While Failing

I am flailing
failing
failing.
Pushing against the current to succeed,
but all I accomplish to end up downstream
farther
and farther
then I had been before.
I don't much sleep
and I over or under eat.
All I want is to
make good by you
but I am failing myself too.
Feeling like I'm trapped in a box
and I've run out of luck,
all expended by finding you.
Which should be enough for me
but here I am on my knees.
I am failing
flailing
failing
you.
Here's a shot in the dark,

pluck me up like a broken lark
and mend these broken wings
because all I want to do is sing
for you
for me.

Sight

Where we go,
we go eyes open
together.

Where we go,
is a future
I never thought
I would have,
but we go eyes open,
together.

Where we go,
with you by my side
we will find
each other.
Eyes open,
together.

Anchors Aweigh

They say I should be scared
of the commitment
I am proposing.

They say I should be scared
of tying myself down
with you alone.

They say I should be scared
of this future I never
knew I needed until I met you.

But what they don't say
is I've set my anchor
and I'll never want to
retrieve it,
for only you
can help me
weather this storm,
forever,
together.

You Said Yes

It was far from traditional
so fitting for us, love
but you said yes.

You picked it out yourself,
and I had nothing fancy to say,
but you said yes.

I planned this all out
and shut it all down,
but you said yes.

It was only August second
and in such a quaint Alaskan town,
but you said yes.

We've had our fights
and we've had our quarrels
but you said yes.

I'll never forget this
and I'm the happiest I've been
because you said yes.

I Won't Give You Away

I just really wanna be with you
and take the time to see this through
I know the things that you can do
I'm following your plan
getting dizzy 'cause we finally did it,
dried ink on the page, now we're committed.
Gotta be the one, I feel prophetic
gave all my gimmicks away

Gave all my gimmicks away
just to be with you.
And I'd toss away more
if you asked me to.
But you don't, that's how good you are.
I'm following your plan, it's mine too
but made all the better with your addition.
Dried ink on the page, now we're to be committed
and I won't ever give that away.

Now we're seeing this through
and I'm all dizzy because we're doing it
the best I've ever had
the best I've ever had

I feel prophetic
but you are definitely the one
you are the one
and I'll never give you away.

We are a Team

I chose you yesterday.
I choose you today.
I will choose you tomorrow and always.
We are imperfect people,
but perfect for each other.
You're my best friend,
my forever and always.
The voices in my head
say nasty things.
But you make them whisper.
You've given me so much
and what do you ask for in return?
Falling in love with you
was like finding the missing puzzle piece
You're my first choice
yesterday
today
tomorrow
forever.
We are a team.

Myself

I try to run away
from who I used to be
but I'm too slow.
The patterns emerge
like mold over me.
The jealousy
the insecurity
the self-doubt.
I think I'm just
another man to you
but it's not true.
I try to run away
from who I used to be,
but I'm too slow.
I just want to prove
I'm not him
anymore.
but I'm failing
failing
failing
for myself
for you
for us.

I think you'd be better off
with someone else.
because my love,
I'm a mess.
but I hope
it's not true.

Closer Than Yesterday

I can wait for years if I gotta
heaven knows I ain't getting over you.
We're not so different
that we won't make this work

Sometimes I feel like
I'm just a man to you,
but you're everything to me.
and I know it isn't true
and I know that puts pressure on you
But that's not my intention,
I promise.

I can wait for years if I gotta
heaven knows I ain't getting over you
So let's pretend
and remember when we were not so different.
Would you say I'm worthy?
Because you're worthy to me.

Sometimes I feel like…
No, let's not even go down that road.
These voices are liars
and I know this is love.

Weigh me down
I can take it.
Weigh me down,

you're my rock against the storm.

One day,
I'll marry you